The science in...

...a piece of PAPER

The science of materials and more...

Camilla de la Bedoyere

W

FRANKLIN WATTS

LONDON•SYDNEY

First published in 2008
by Franklin Watts

Copyright © Franklin Watts 2008

Franklin Watts
338 Euston Road
London NW1 3BH

Franklin Watts Australia
Level 17/207 Kent Street
Sydney, NSW 2000

Planning and production by
Discovery Books Limited
Editor: Rebecca Hunter
Designer: Keith Williams
Illustrator: Stefan Chabluk
Photo researcher: Tom Humphrey

Dewey number 620.1'1

ISBN 978 0 7496 8240 8

Printed in China

Franklin Watts is a division of Hachette
Children's Books, an Hachette Livre UK
company. www.hachettelivre.co.uk

Photo acknowledgements: Getty Images/Steve Gorton, front cover top; istockphoto.com, front cover bottom left & bottom right; istockphoto.com/Wendy Shiao, front cover bottom middle; istockphoto.com/Christopher Festi, p. 4; istockphoto.com/Linda Steward, p. 5 top; istockphoto.com, p. 5 bottom; istockphoto.com/Olga Shelego, p. 6; Corbis/Araldo de Luca, p. 8; Corbis/Brooklyn Museum, p. 9; Rebecca Hunter, p. 10; istockphoto.com, p. 11 top; istockphoto.com/Hywit Dimyadi, p. 11 bottom; Corbis/Doug Wilson, p. 12; Corbis/Natalie Fobes, p. 13 top; istockphoto.com, p. 13 bottom; www.arcticpaper.com, p. 14 bottom; istockphoto.com/Max Blain, p. 14 top; Science Photo Library/David R. Frazier, p. 15 top; Science Photo Library/Kaj R. Svensson, p. 15 bottom; Corbis/Louis Psihoyos, p. 16; istockphoto.com/Anna Yu, p. 17; istockphoto.com/Piotr Sikora, p. 18 top; istockphoto.com, p. 18 bottom; istockphoto.com/Tony Tremblay, p. 19 top; istockphoto.com/Wendy Shiao, p. 19 bottom; Corbis/Bettmann, p. 22; istockphoto.com/David H. Lewis, p. 23 top; istockphoto.com, p. 23 bottom; istockphoto.com, p. 24; istockphoto.com/Bryan Boucher, p. 25 top; CFW Images/Edward Parker, p. 25 bottom; Corbis/Lester Lefkowitz, p. 26; Getty Images/Justin Sullivan, p. 27 top; istockphoto.com, p. 27 bottom; istockphoto.com/Bennie Jacobs, p. 28; istockphoto.com, p. 29 top; Corbis/Alan Schein, p. 29 bottom

Contents

Words that appear in **bold**
are in the glossary on page 30.

Perfect paper

If paper had never been invented our world would be a very different place to live in. Imagine: no books, no newspapers, no paper money!

Thankfully, our ancestors came up with the brilliant notion of mashing wood up into a mushy **pulp**, and turning it into thin sheets that they could write on. It was a remarkable discovery, and one that has changed the course of human history.

This book (which is made of paper, of course) will explain just how

wonderful, and important, a simple piece of paper can be. You will also learn where paper comes from, how it is made – and all about its past, present and future.

▼ *Colourful paper dragons are used in Chinese New Year parades.*

▲ *The first sticky, paper postage stamps came into use in Britain in 1840. These American stamps date from 1965.*

Paper records

Paper has been around for a long time because it is perfect for the tasks we need it for. We can write, print or draw on paper and our words and pictures can become a permanent record of our thoughts and experiences. It is thanks to paper that we know so much about people who lived long ago. They wrote things down, and now we can read their stories, and enjoy their art.

▼ *Books are probably the most important item made of paper worldwide.*

A thousand uses

Paper has other uses too. You can carry your groceries in a paper bag, put letters in paper envelopes, use paper tissues to wipe your nose, buy things with paper banknotes – you can even make planes with it!

It is possible to change paper into something else. Sticking lots of layers of paper together, for example, makes cardboard, which is tough and hard-wearing. When a sheet of paper is no longer needed, it can even be mashed up again, and turned into new paper.

Paper is a material

Everything is made from a material, or a combination of materials. Glass, paper and plastics are all types of material. The 'properties' of a material are its characteristics, and how it is useful to us.

Paper properties

Here are some of the most useful properties of paper:

- It can be folded or bent
- It can be made huge or tiny
- It can be torn or cut
- It burns
- It is lightweight
- It can be different colours
- It can be different thicknesses
- Ink and glue stick to it
- It can be made into lots of different shapes.

Paper problems

Paper has its uses, but there are some things it wouldn't be good for. You would not use this material to build with, for example. Paper is flimsy, not sturdy. It is weak, not tough – and it **absorbs**, or soaks up, water very easily. You cannot use paper near fire, as it burns.

It is possible to change paper's properties, though. Other materials can be added to it during **production** to make it stronger, or waterproof. A paper cup sounds like a bad idea –

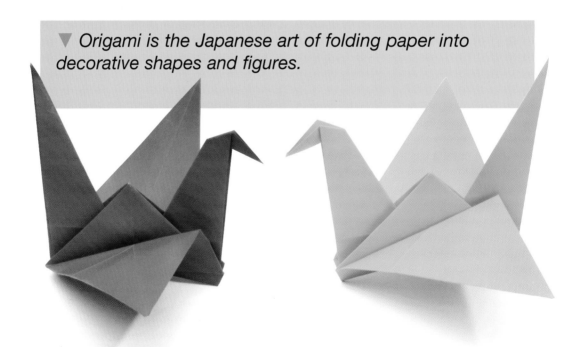

▼ *Origami is the Japanese art of folding paper into decorative shapes and figures.*

you might expect liquid to seep through the paper. In fact, these cups work because they are coated with thin layers of plastic or wax inside. This makes the paper waterproof.

Fold, fold and fold again

Take an ordinary sheet of paper and fold it in half, then half again. Keep folding it in half, until you can't fold it any more. How many folds did you manage?

What happens if you use a bigger piece of paper? Do you think you will be able to make more folds? Try it and see.

Predict what would happen if you used a thinner piece of paper.

▶ *Just a thought... If you have tried the paper folding exercise above, you will know there is a limit to the number of times you can fold a piece of paper. But just suppose there was no limit, and that you had an enormous piece of paper and the means to fold it as many times as you wanted. Can you imagine how thick it would be after 5 folds? 10 folds? The results would actually amaze you!*

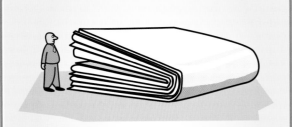

If you could fold it 15 times the piece of paper would be as tall as a person.

Just five more folds, and it would be the height of a tall building.

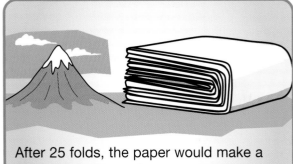

After 25 folds, the paper would make a mountain look small.

If paper could be folded 50 times it would be bigger than our planet.

Paper in the past

Long ago, in a region of the world that was once called Sumer – now southern Iraq – a system for writing language developed. Words and meanings were recorded by making symbols and marks in wet clay tablets. When dry, the tablets could be passed from hand to hand, and the messages read. Most of them contained information about the buying and selling of goods.

Set in stone

Writing on clay had its advantages. Once they had set dry, the marks couldn't be changed, so no one could argue about what had been agreed. The tablets formed permanent records and many of them, thousands of years old, survive today.

▲ *A stone tablet bearing ancient writing symbols.*

Timeline

3500 BCE The first writing system, with more than 700 symbols, was developing in Sumer.

3000 BCE Papyrus was being made in ancient Egypt.

200-300 BCE Parchment is invented.

105 CE Ts'ai Lun invents modern paper in China.

700-800 CE Paper making reaches Central Asia.

1300-1400 CE Mills for making paper are set up across Europe.

1430s CE Printing is invented, increasing demand for paper.

1800s CE Paper-making machinery is invented.

Papyrus

In ancient Egypt, people made good use of a plant that grows along the banks of the River Nile. Papyrus is a reed with tough threads, or **fibres**. The fibres were removed and arranged side by side to make one layer. The next layer was laid at right angles, and so on. As the fibres dried, the **sap** of the plant acted like glue.

▲ *The fibres from reeds are laid in sheets to form papyrus. Alternate layers are arranged so the fibres lie in different directions. This makes the material tough.*

Parchment

Animal skins have also been used as a writing material, called **parchment**. The skin of dead goats, sheep and cows was scraped, stretched and dried. It could take many animal skins to produce enough parchment for a single book.

Paper is invented

Modern paper was invented nearly 2,000 years ago in China by Ts'ai Lun. He made a sheet of paper using wood from a mulberry tree, which he mixed with other materials, such as rags and old fishing nets.

From rags to pulp

It wasn't until the 1800s that paper makers stopped using rags and developed ways of pulping wood. Since then, scientists have developed even better ways of making paper quickly and cheaply.

◄ *Papyrus gave us the word 'paper' and it was the most common writing material in ancient times. Unlike clay tablets, it was lightweight and portable (easy to carry). Stories and events were recorded on papyrus in ancient Egyptian times.*

Paper from trees

The main ingredient of paper is wood pulp, which comes from timber. Since trees are part of the natural environment their timber is called a natural or raw material. People make, or manufacture, paper from timber – so it is called a man-made material.

Timber

The wood from trees is called timber, and there are two main types: softwood and hardwood. Softwood timber usually comes from conifer trees and it is easy to cut. Conifers are evergreen trees with soft, needle-like leaves and seed-bearing cones. Hardwood comes from **deciduous** trees.

Wood contains tough fibres made of cellulose that are perfect for making paper with. Cellulose is one of the most abundant materials on Earth, since it is found in all plants. It helps keep a plant's cells stiff and strong. The fibres of cellulose are bound together by **lignin**, another plant-building material.

▼ *Piles of newly-cut timber waiting to be transported to their destination at a paper mill.*

▼ A paper wasp protects its carefully constructed nest.

Paper from plants

All plants, not just trees, contain cellulose fibres. In places where trees do not grow in large numbers paper can be made from the pulp of other plants, such as straw, bamboo and sugar cane (below).

Wasps make paper too

Some types of wasps live in large groups, or colonies. They make their nests from wood pulp.

It is a simple process: a wasp uses its mouthparts, or mandibles, to scrape wood fibres from any available source such as fences, fallen trees, cardboard boxes and telegraph poles. The wasp chews the fibres into pulp, mixing them with saliva (spit). As they are chewed, the fibres turn into a paste, which the wasp adds to the nest structure. The saliva acts like glue, binding the pulp together. Once dry, the paper nest is very tough and durable (long-lasting).

Forest to factory

About half of the trees that are cut down to make paper are grown in managed forests, where they are harvested like a crop. The other half comes from wood fibre, from sawmills, vegetable matter and recycled paper and cloth.

Which wood?

Most trees used for paper making are softwood trees such as spruce, pine and fir. The cellulose fibres in softwood trees are quite long (2-4 mm) and make good, strong paper. Hardwood trees such as oak, poplar and elm have shorter fibres (0.5-1.5 mm), so paper made from this timber is weaker. Hardwood trees take much longer to grow than softwoods, so their wood is more expensive.

Paper makers often use a mixture of hardwoods and softwoods to create the perfect blend for the material they are manufacturing. They need to think about what the paper will be used for, and the properties they want it to have. Hardwood trees make a smoother paper – so it is a better choice for writing and printing.

It is the job of forestry workers to plant new **saplings** and look after them; young trees have to be protected from animals, pests and disease. When the trees are the right size, they are felled using saws and cut into logs. At this stage, the timber is called **lumber**.

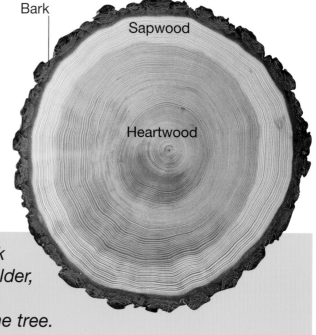

Bark
Sapwood
Heartwood

► *A cross section of a tree. The dark centre is called heartwood – this is older, dead wood. The light wood is called sapwood and is the living wood in the tree. If you counted all the rings in this cross section, you would have some idea of how old the tree is – one ring for each year of growth.*

▲ *A logger cuts up timber in the Tongass National Forest, Alaska, USA.*

On the road

The lumber is removed from the forest by various means depending on what methods of transport are available – trucks, tractors or railway wagons. In very remote areas, such as parts of Scandinavia and Canada, timber is often floated down rivers to factories or harbour ports. In South-east Asia elephants were once used to drag lumber out of the forests.

Of all the world's wood harvest, about 40 per cent of it is turned into pulp for making paper. This figure is expected to increase.

▼ *Timber is loaded on to large lorries for its journey to the paper mill.*

13

Lumber to pulp

Paper-making factories or mills are often located near rivers. This is because the paper-making process uses huge quantities of water and also because, historically, rivers were a useful means of transport.

When the lumber reaches the mill, it needs to be prepared. It will go through a series of machines that will change the raw material into something quite different.

First the logs are tumbled in a drum to remove their bark. Then they are sent to chipping machines that cut the wood into tiny woodchips. Woodchips can be turned into pulp using one of two methods: mechanical or chemical pulping.

▲ *A chipping machine turns logs into piles of woodchips, ready for pulping.*

◀ *The Arctic paper mill in Kostrzyn, Poland is located on the banks of a river.*

Mechanical pulping

The woodchips are shredded into small pieces using a mechanical grinder. As they pass through the grinder they are forced between turning grindstones with **abrasive** surfaces. This process separates the wood fibres, and breaks them into smaller lengths. A lot of water is added at this stage to make a slushy pulp. The pulp from mechanical processes is called groundwood pulp. It produces weak paper that discolours easily. This is often used to make newspaper.

Chemical pulping

In the chemical pulping process, woodchips are put into large tanks, called digesters. Here they are boiled at high pressure in a solution of sodium hydroxide and sodium sulphide. These chemicals make the lignin **soluble** so the wood chips **dissolve** into pulp in the solution.

▲ *This wood pulp slurry has been **bleached**, which is why it is so white.*

▼ *Modern digesters contain a pulpy mixture of chemicals and woodchips. They may be more than 60 metres tall and can produce 600 tonnes of pulp every day.*

Pulp to paper

In order to make paper from the liquid pulp, several other processes are required. The water must be removed from the pulp and then it must be dried. Other materials can be added which alter the type of paper that is produced.

Bleaching

First the pulp is washed and bleach is added to remove any colour and whiten the fibres. At this stage the mixture of wood fibres and liquid is called a stock.

Beating

The stock now goes into a machine called a 'beater' where the fibres are pounded, squeezed and mashed. Different materials may be added to the mixture at this stage that will make the paper suitable for its final use.

- **Rags** – Cotton and linen are fabrics that can be shredded to fibres, and added to wood fibres to make tough, long-lasting paper.

- **Waste paper** – Recycled paper can be pulped and added to the mix. It has to be cleaned to remove old ink and dirt.

- **Man-made, or synthetic**, fibres can be added to the pulp. The addition of rayon fibres, for example, make a stronger paper.

- **Fillers** – Chemicals such as calcium carbonate and china clay are added to paper to increase its brightness or surface smoothness. Fillers and other chemicals also help ink to stick to paper.

- **Pigments or dyes** can be added to the paper stock to make coloured paper.

Crayons, hairspray, ink, paint, nail varnish, cycle helmets and shaving cream are just some of the many products that can be made from the from the by-products (leftovers) of the paper-making process.

Pulp spray

Before the fibres can be turned into paper, the liquid needs to be removed from the pulp. The beaten stock is sprayed onto a large, moving belt of fine mesh screening. The water drains out of the bottom, and is collected to be reused. The pulp is squeezed through a series of rollers to remove the water.

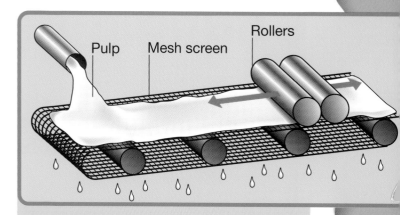

▲ *Paper pulp is poured onto a screen and rolled to remove the water.*

Press and dry

At this stage, the pulpy paper still contains about 60 per cent water. It moves on to the press section of the machine where it is pressed between rollers of wool felt. Then it is passed over a series of steam-heated cylinders that heat the wet sheets and force the fibres closer together. As they are packed tighter, the fibres dry and become paper. Finally the paper is wound onto large reels where it will be processed further depending on what its end use is.

▼ *The finished paper is rolled onto a reel, ready for transport or cutting.*

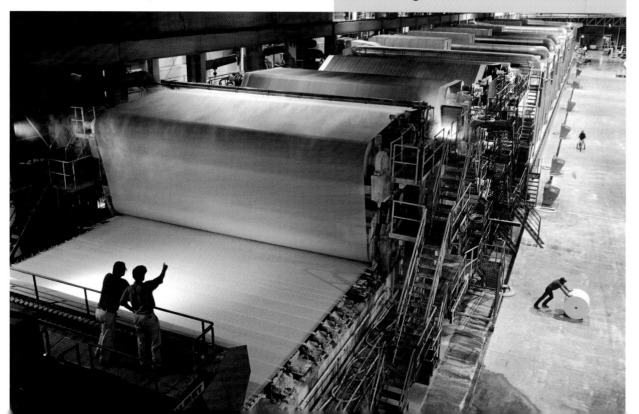

Changing paper

Paper is a material that can be adapted and changed, so its properties suit its functions, or uses.

Banknotes

Banknotes, or bills, are usually made with paper that is toughened with cotton or other fabric fibres. They may contain special security features, such as threads or **watermarks** so they are difficult to copy, or counterfeit. Some countries use plastic banknotes.

Sandpaper

Grains of sand, or other tough materials, can be glued to paper to produce an abrasive surface. Sandpaper is used to smooth other materials, such as wood.

▼ *Paper banknotes were first used in the 7th century, in China. These notes called Euros were introduced to Europe in 2002.*

▼ *Photos are printed on special paper that creates a shiny, long-lasting image.*

Photographic paper

Paper used for photographs needs to have special coatings. These are usually glossy and help ink to stay in place without spreading sideways.

▲ *Cardboard boxes are tough, cheap and lightweight. They can be stacked, squashed and recycled.*

Card

Layers of paper can be glued to one another to make card. If a layer is glued in a wavy pattern, corrugated cardboard is produced. Card and cardboard are strong enough to be used for packing and carrying things.

Prints

Wallpaper and wrapping paper have colours and patterns printed onto the surface. Vinyl wallpaper has a thin coat of plastic so it can be wiped clean.

Reams of paper

Paper can be made of different weights. Tissue paper is obviously lighter than brown paper. Sheets of paper are counted in reams, no matter what the weight or type. One ream normally contains 500 sheets.

Changing properties

Look back at the list of paper properties on page 6, and write a list of properties for wood. Can you find some properties that change when wood is made into paper, and some that stay the same? Think about the properties of thick card. Is card similar to wood, or paper – or both? What are the properties of tissue paper that make it useful?

Tissue

Tissue paper, napkins, paper towels and facial wipes are made to be very absorbent. They are dried and folded at the same time, keeping the fibres loose, with pockets of air between them that can trap and hold liquid.

▲ *Tissue paper and card can be made in many different bright colours.*

Making paper

Early paper makers didn't need a paper mill with machinery to get good results, and nor do you. You can make paper as long as you get the right equipment together first. It is a messy job, though, so be prepared!

You will need:

A screen, which you can get from a craft shop, or make from a wooden frame and stiff net curtain fabric. Staple the fabric to the frame so it is really tight.

Waste paper e.g. newspaper, tissue paper   Large tray   Wooden spoon

Mixing bowl   Kitchen towels

Hot water   Rolling pin

Whisk or electric blender   Food colouring

Method

1 Tear the paper into small pieces (about 2.5 cm x 2.5 cm) and put them in a bowl. Add hot water and mix well. Leave this mixture overnight.

2 Tear the mushy paper into even smaller pieces and whisk by hand or blend in an electric blender to loosen the fibres and make a pulp. You can add a few drops of food colouring at this stage.

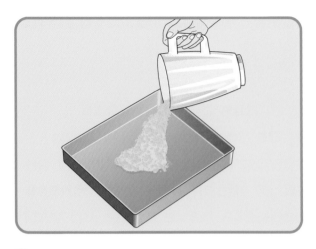

3 Pour the pulp into a large tray and make a stock by adding just enough water to cover the paper.

4 Prepare a thick pad of kitchen towels on a table.

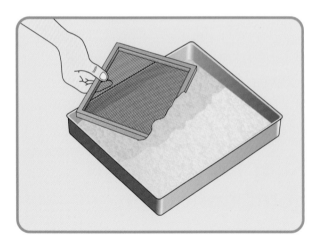

5 Put your screen into the tray and swish it around, collecting pulp on the top. You can use your hands to add pulp to any gaps. Lift the screen and let the water drain away.

6 Carefully flip your screen onto the kitchen towels, and tap it gently until the layer of paper comes away.

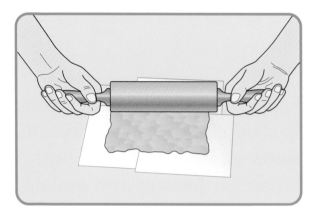

7 Use a rolling pin to flatten the paper and squeeze out some water. Leave your paper overnight, as it has to dry thoroughly before it is ready to use.

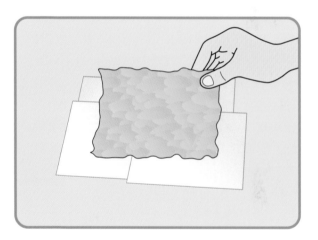

Next time you can add glitter, coloured tissue, rose petals or perfume to the stock to create different effects.

Paper from dung

It is possible to make paper from elephant dung. It needs to be boiled and steamed so all the bacteria are killed, before it is mashed into a pulp. Don't try this one at home!

Keeping records

Paper is an important material: it has changed the course of civilization by allowing us to record our own history. Books, maps and newspapers have all played an essential part in the development of ideas. Because these items are so precious to us, scientists have come up with ways to preserve, or save, these records for the future.

A great scientist and artist

Leonardo da Vinci (1452-1519) was one of the world's greatest thinkers and artists. He lived in Italy during the Renaissance – a period of time in history when new ideas about art, culture and science were becoming important. Da Vinci kept records of all his thoughts and drawings in notebooks, which he carried with him everywhere. He understood the importance of carefully looking at, or observing nature, and scribbled down thousands of pages of notes. He also completed sketches, many of which survive today. Modern scientists still use da Vinci's methods of observation and record-keeping.

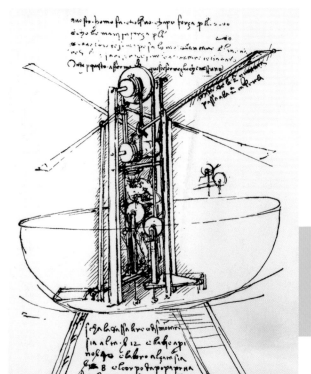

Keeping paper in good condition

Like other natural materials, paper can rot and suffer damage. Keeping important historical records in good condition is a science called paper **conservation**.

◀ *One of Leonardo da Vinci's amazing designs. He kept detailed records of all his inventions and thoughts written down on paper.*

Brown spots can appear on ancient records. They are caused by a **mould** and can be prevented by storing paper at the right temperature and **humidity**. Booklice, silverfish and carpet beetles are bugs that feed on books, the glue that binds them and their covers. Book pests can be prevented by storing books in dry, dark places and keeping them clean.

Printing on paper

By the middle of the 15th century the printing press had been invented. Johannes Gutenberg (c.1398-1468) from Germany is credited with inventing the method of mechanical printing. One of the first books he printed was the Bible. Two hundred copies of the Gutenberg Bible were printed. About fifty of them survive today.

▲ *Libraries store books, magazines and maps that can be used and enjoyed by everyone in the community.*

The immediate effect of the printing press was to cut the costs of making books and to make them available to a much larger segment of the population. Libraries could now store greater quantities of information at a much lower cost. Printing could spread new ideas quickly and with greater impact.

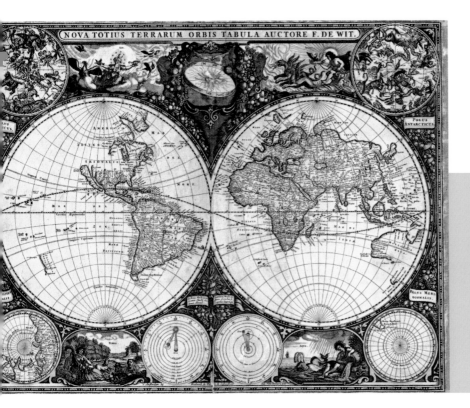

◄ *Maps helped early explorers and traders to visit places and discover new areas. Measurements of journey times, coastlines and other details were recorded on paper and drawings were made to help sailors navigate the high seas.*

Environment matters

Paper comes from a natural resource – trees – that can be replaced. When one tree is felled for lumber, another can be grown in its place. However, like all natural resources, we should take care of forests so they are around forever.

Forests are the future

Forests are not just a source of timber, they are living, thriving **ecosystems**, where millions of animals and plants exist together. Even when a single tree is cut down, animals and plants that depend on it will be affected.

If we use more paper, it will be necessary to plant more forests to supply the paper-making **industry**. That might mean cutting down natural forests, with lots of different types of trees and plants growing in them, and replacing them with large plantations of one type of tree, such as pine. This means we would lose natural ecosystems.

▼ *A natural woodland takes thousands of years to grow and develop. It contains a rich mixture of life, including mammals, birds, insects, reptiles and flowering plants.*

A breath of fresh air

Forests are called the lungs of the world. Trees produce **oxygen** – the gas that humans and other animals breathe. They also absorb **carbon dioxide**, a gas that is thought to contribute to **global warming**.

▲ *Rows of identical trees, grown in huge plantations, do not support a wide range of wildlife. However, they are good sources of lumber.*

One down, one up

In Canada, forestry managers are obliged by law to replace every single tree they cut down. This will help efforts to reduce the amount of carbon dioxide in the Earth's atmosphere.

▶ *Conifers are grown and felled in huge numbers to support the worldwide need for timber to make paper.*

Reduce, reuse, recycle

The best way to save the world's forests is to reduce the amount of paper we use, reuse paper whenever possible, and recycle it when we have finished with it. This also helps cut down the amount of energy that is used in making and transporting paper.

Reduce

You can reduce your waste paper by:

- Using email
- Collecting paper that has been used on one side to make notebooks
- Keeping scraps of paper by the telephone for taking messages, or using them for writing shopping lists
- Only printing documents you really need
- Using narrower margins and a smaller font size when you print.

Recycling one tonne of paper can save
- 19 trees
- 29,400 litres of water
- 30 kg of **pollution**
- 2.7 cubic metres of **landfill**.
It also saves enough energy to power a home for more than six months!

Reuse

Use your imagination and you will find ways to reuse paper. You can:

- Use both sides of a piece of paper
- Use newspaper to make paper chains
- Use a piece of wrapping paper again
- Save your Christmas and birthday cards to make gift tags from them.

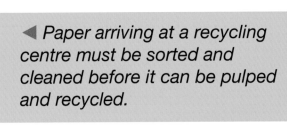

◀ *Paper arriving at a recycling centre must be sorted and cleaned before it can be pulped and recycled.*

▶ *Newspapers are often made from recycled paper.*

Recycle

Recycled paper can be used to make lots of things, such as:

- **Insulation**: recycled newspaper can be turned into a material for insulating buildings
- Fuel: waste paper can be made into pellets and burnt to release energy (for example, to produce electricity)
- Paper products: printing and writing paper, newspapers, toilet paper, kitchen towels, etc.

Burn and bury

Waste paper that is put in rubbish bins is likely to be burned in **incinerators**, or buried in landfill sites. Both of these methods pollute the environment. Around 25 per cent of waste in British bins is paper, most of which could have been recycled instead.

▼ *Unsorted rubbish is dumped in landfill sites. Many countries are now running out of space to put landfill waste.*

The future of paper

Paper has been around for about 2,000 years. Will it still be used another 2,000 years from now? No one knows, but even today – in the electronic age of computers, emails, telephones and instant messaging – the demand for paper continues to increase.

Plastic – the new paper?

In recent years plastic – a synthetic material – has replaced paper in many ways. Plastic bags and containers, for example, are usually tougher and more durable than paper ones. They also have the advantage of being waterproof.

Over the last 20 years the worldwide demand for paper and paper products has doubled, and it is expected to carry on increasing.

Plastic problems

Plastic, however, is made from oil – which is a resource that we will run out of one day. Furthermore, plastic and other synthetic materials, such as polystyrene, do not break up easily and may stay in landfill sites for centuries, causing pollution.

◀ *Playing cards are usually made from paper. What materials could be used to replace paper for this purpose? What advantages, or disadvantages, might a different material have?*

E-books

Can you imagine a book with no paper? Electronic books (or e-books) are being developed that will allow a person to read books on a handheld device or download them onto a personal computer. E-books could prove to be much cheaper than ordinary books. They will save paper and storage space too.

▲ *Computers may help the modern student and schoolchild, but paper and pens are still essential tools for most people.*

A perfect, popular product

Whatever the future holds for paper, it is hard to imagine a better material to use for scribbling down a quick note or sketch. It is cheap, easy to make, lightweight and comes from a natural resource that can be replaced.

Look around your home and school for products that are made from paper. Now you can think about it as a material: its properties and its uses. How different would our world be without this brilliant invention?

▼ *Ticker tape parades began in New York in 1886 when the Statue of Liberty was dedicated. During celebrations, hundreds of tonnes of shredded office paper are traditionally thrown from windows onto the street.*

Glossary

abrasive rough or harsh

absorb soak up liquid

bleached caused a material, such as paper, to become white by using a chemical process

carbon dioxide the gas that we breathe out during respiration, and that plants need so they can release energy from sunlight in the process we call photosynthesis

conservation the treatment of materials to help extend their survival and usefulness

deciduous trees that lose their leaves in winter

dissolve for a solid to become part of a liquid

ecosystem the close relationship between the living things in an environment

fibre a thread-like substance that makes up a material

global warming the way the temperature of the Earth's atmosphere is increasing

humidity the amount of water in the air

incinerator a large piece of equipment in which waste matter is burnt

industry the process of turning raw materials into products, or making products in factories

insulation materials that are good at keeping heat in or out

landfill a place where waste matter is dumped and buried

lignin a substance found in the cells of plants. It makes the stems of plants rigid and woody

lumber timber that has been partly prepared for use in industry

mould a type of fungus

oxygen the gas we need to breathe, and the gas that plants produce when they release energy from sunlight

parchment a paper-like material made from the skin of animals

pollution harmful substances that have been released into the environment

production the process of making, or manufacturing, things

pulp the substance made when timber has been mashed with water

sap the liquid that moves around inside plants. Sap carries sugar and minerals to all parts of the plant

sapling a young tree

soluble able to be dissolved

synthetic a man-made material

watermark a faint design on paper that is visible when it is held against the light

Further information

Websites

www.kbears.com/sciences

Check out this science website for some fun and games.

www.robertsabuda.com/ popupindex.asp

Find out about pop up books and how to make them.

www.kidsrecycle.org

Investigate ways to recycle at school and home.

www.bbc.co.uk/schools

Click on 'science' where you will find Digger and his Gang waiting to share their adventures.

www.kids.nationalgeographic.com

A brilliant science site that covers all aspects of our natural world.

www.strangematterexhibit.com

Discover science activities and challenges.

Note to parents and teachers: Every effort has been made by the publishers to ensure that these websites are suitable for children, that they are of the highest educational value, and that they contain no inappropriate or offensive material. However, because of the nature of the Internet, it is impossible to guarantee that the contents of these sites will not be altered. We strongly advise that Internet access is supervised by a responsible adult.

Index